The Three L...

A Publication of the World Language Division

Director of Product Development: Judith M. Bittinger

Executive Editor: Elinor Chamas

Editorial Development: Elly Schottman

Production/Manufacturing: James W. Gibbons

Cover and Text Design/Art Direction: Taurins Design
Associates, New York

Illustrator: Diane Teske Harris

ISBN 0-201-19058-3

17 18 19 20-WR-99 98 97

Addison-Wesley Publishing Company

Once upon a time,
there were three little pigs.
The first little pig built
a house out of straw.

The second little pig built
a house out of wood.
The third little pig built
a house out of bricks.

4

The Wolf knocked at the
door of the first little pig.

Little pig, little pig,
let me in, let me in.

Not by the hair on my
chinny-chin-chin!

Then I'll **huff,** and I'll **puff,**
and I'll **blow** your house in.

The Wolf huffed
and he puffed
and he blew the house in.

6

The Wolf knocked at the door of the second little pig.

Little pig, little pig, let me in, let me in.

Not by the hair on my chinny-chin-chin!

Then I'll **huff,** and I'll **puff,** and I'll **blow** your house in.

The Wolf huffed
and he puffed
and he blew the house in.

The Wolf knocked at the door of the third little pig.

Little pig, little pig,
let me in, let me in.

Not by the hair on my chinny-chin-chin!

Then I'll **huff,** and I'll **puff,** and I'll **blow** your house in!

But the Wolf could not blow in the house of the third little pig.

So the Wolf climbed up
on the roof.
Ha, ha, ha!
I'll go down the chimney.

But the third little pig
had a big pot of soup
on the fire.

The Wolf landed
right in the soup.

12

The Wolf jumped out of
the pot of soup.
He ran out the door
and down the hill.

And the three little pigs
never saw the Wolf again.

The End